Discover Jainism

Colin Hynson

Series Editor
Mehool H Sanghrajka

London

2 What is Jainism?

Jainism is an ancient faith that comes from India. Alongside Hinduism, Islam and Sikhism it is still one of the most important faiths in modern India. Today Jains live all over the world and there are many Jains who have made Britain their home. Jains share many beliefs with both Buddhists and Hindus. Like both of these faiths, Jains believe in reincarnation. That means that when we die our soul is born again in a new body and carries on in another life. This does not have to be another person but could also be an animal or even a plant. Jains believe that by living each life as well as possible the soul will eventually be freed from this cycle of birth, death and rebirth. Neither Jains nor Buddhists believe in any god or goddess as the creator of the universe.

Respect for All Things

Jains believe that all living things have a soul within them. For Jains each of these souls has an equal value and should be treated with respect and compassion. This means that Jains should be strict vegetarians. They should also try to live in a way that does not damage the world in which they live.

This Jain temple was built in Potters Bar, Hertfordshire in August 2005. It is one of several temples that serve the Jain community in London.

Birth, Death and Rebirth

The aim of every Jain is to liberate their soul from continually being reincarnated. This can only be done by following what are called the 'Three Jewels' of Jainism. These mean believing in the right things, having a proper knowledge of the world and living a proper life. All three have to be followed if the soul is to be finally freed.

Two Sects

Jains are divided into two major groups or sects. These are the Digambara (which means 'clothed in the sky') and the Svetambara (which means 'clothed in white'). Both groups agree on all of the basic beliefs of Jainism. Their disagreements are mostly about how Jain monks and nuns should live. Both sects got their names because of their different ideas about the clothes that monks should wear. The Digambaras believe that monks should be naked (or 'clothed in the sky') whilst the Svetambara monks can wear simple white clothes.

These Jain monks are Svetambara because they are dressed in white robes. Here they are being offered food and water by a householder.

How many Jains are there?

There are about 10 million Jains living in India. However, the total population of India is just over 1 billion. This means that the Jains represent about 1% of India's total population. There are an estimated 30,000 Jains living in Britain today.

These elephants are being used during a Jain procession. Jains believe that when the elephants and the people riding them die then they will be reincarnated.

www.learnjainism.org

4 The Birth of Jainism

Jains believe that their faith has been around for as long as the universe has existed. Jains also believe that the universe itself is eternal and has never had a beginning. For Jains this means that Jainism has no beginning either. It has simply always been in existence. However, Jains think that the truth about Jainism is revealed at different times by special people called 'tirthankaras'. They are teachers who 'make a ford' or show the way. Other faiths would call them prophets. Each tirthankara is somebody who has reached a state where they have full knowledge of their soul. He can then teach others how to get to the same goal.

The Tirthankaras

According to Jains there have been 24 tirthankaras in this half of the current time cycle. The first Tirthankara was called Adinatha. Jains believe he lived millions of years ago and regard him as the first person to bring Jainism to the people of India and who helped to develop agriculture, commerce and the arts. Svetambaras believe that the 19th Tirthankara, Malli, was a woman. Digambaras disagree and say that a woman cannot become a tirthankara. There is some evidence for the existence of the 23rd Tirthankara. His name was Parshva. He lived in about 800 BC. Many of the principles of modern Jainism can be traced back to Parshva.

An image of the 16th Tirthankara, Shantinath, at the Victoria and Albert Museum in London.

Mahavira

This girl is praying to a richly decorated statue of Mahavira in a Jain temple in South London.

The 24th (and last) Tirthankara was Mahavira. He was born in about 600 BC and his parents named him Vardhamana. He was the son of King Siddhartha and Queen Trishala. His family were followers of the teachings of Parshva. When he was about 30 years old Mahavira left the palace where he lived and began to live a simple life without any pleasures or comforts. For the next 12 years he spent his time fasting and meditating. At the end of this he reached a full understanding of his soul. He then spent the rest of his life teaching others and made Jainism more popular. The title Mahavira means 'great hero'.

The Expansion of Jainism

Mahavira was born in northeast India in the modern state of Bihar.

Mahavira achieved liberation (or moksha) in about 527 BC. Jains believe that after liberation a soul does not need to enter another body. After his liberation Jainism grew slowly. Many people in India were becoming Buddhists and the Jains remained as a small group. In about 300 BC an Indian emperor called Chandragupta Maurya was converted to Jainism by a monk called Bhadrabahu. Chandragupta Maurya ruled over one of the most powerful empires in India. When he converted to Jainism he gave up his throne and lived as a Jain monk until his death. His conversion meant that the Jain faith could begin to spread throughout this empire.

6 The Religions of India

As Jainism began to spread throughout India it had to face two other great faiths. Hinduism had gained popularity in India for many centuries before Mahavira began his teachings. Mahavira also began his teaching at about the same time as an Indian prince called Siddhartha Gautama began to spread the word about a new faith which became known as Buddhism. All three of these faiths influenced each other in lots of different ways. Some of the early Hindu and Buddhist texts mention some of the Jain tirthankaras.

The Arrival of Hinduism

A giant statue of Shiva in India. Shiva is one of the most important gods in the Hindu religion.

The word Hindu comes from the river Indus and it means the people who live near the Indus river. It is believed that in about 1500 BC a group of people known as the Aryans arrived in India from the region between southern Russia and central Asia, and settled by the Indus river. The area was already settled by many people. One of the cities in which they lived was called Harappa. These two groups of people had their own religions. These slowly came together to create the faith that we know as Hinduism. By around 600 BC, under the influence of Jainism and Buddhism, the idea of reincarnation began to take hold among Hindus. Three hundred years later Hindus began to stop the practice of sacrificing animals and began to worship two new Gods, Vishnu and Shiva. Neither of these Gods needed animal sacrifices.

The Rig Veda

The first written evidence of Hinduism that we can read is the Rig Veda, a set of hymns probably composed from about 1500 BC to 1000 BC. People sang or recited the Rig Veda for hundreds of years before it was finally written down around 300 BC.

The Rise of Buddhism

Buddhism arose soon after Jainism began to appear in India. The history of Buddhism is really the story of one man, Siddhartha Gautama, who was alive when Mahavira was teaching people about Jainism. Siddhartha Gautama was born around the year 563 BC. He was born into a royal family and lived a life of great wealth and privilege. When he was a young man he went outside the royal palace and saw sickness and suffering for the first time in his life. He decided to leave the life he was leading and to live as a homeless holy man. He wanted to find a way to escape the suffering that he had seen. He decided that this could be done by living a good and pure life so that eventually, after being reincarnated many times, a person's suffering would eventually disappear. Now known as the Buddha, Siddhartha Gautama spent the rest of his life sharing his beliefs with many others. In about 300 BC an Indian king called Asoka became a Buddhist and helped Buddhism to spread across India.

This image of the Buddha was created in the 7th century and comes from eastern India.

8 Reaching Perfection

Just like Buddhists and Hindus, Jains believe in reincarnation. This means that everybody will live more than one life. Whenever a living thing dies then the soul within goes to another body instantly. This does not have to be another human being. It could easily be an animal or even a plant. The soul of a dead animal or plant could also move into the body of a newly born human. The aim for Jains is for their souls to eventually break free from this cycle of birth, death and rebirth. This means getting rid of karma from their souls. Jains believe that they can remove karma from their souls by following the 'Three Jewels' of Jainism. These mean believing in the right things, having a proper knowledge of the world and living a proper life.

Jewel 1 - Believing in the right things

Jains call this 'right faith' (Samyak Darshana). This does not mean that Jains should believe what they have been told. It means being able to understand things properly. Jains should avoid making up their minds before they have seen anything and they should avoid prejudice and superstition. Both of these things will prevent Jains from reaching 'right faith'. It also means having total faith in the teachings of the tirthankaras.

On holy days like Diwali (see page 15) Jain children often dress up and go to the temple

Jewel 2 - Having a Proper Knowledge of the World

Many of the Svetambara scriptures were believed to have been written in Gujarat, western India. This temple was built on the site where these monks helped to write the scriptures.

Jains call this 'right knowledge' (Samyak Jnana). For Jains this means that they have to have an accurate and a sufficient knowledge of the universe in which they live. They must understand the Jain belief that the universe is made up of six 'universal substances'. These are matter, soul, motion, rest, space and time. Jains must understand the seven truths (or 'Tattvas') that exist in the universe. It also means that Jains must understand that all life must be respected.

Jewel 3 - Living a Proper Life

These Jain nuns are busy doing their daily chores. They spend many hours studying the Jain scriptures.

Jains call this 'right conduct' (Samyak Charitra). Jains believe that the amount of karma that is attached to their souls depends on how they behave during their lives. Right faith and right knowledge are needed so that Jains know how to live their lives as well as they can. By taking 'vows' Jains lead a proper life because they minimise the harm they cause to other living beings. Jain monks and nuns have to take five very strict vows on how to live their lives. Ordinary Jains have twelve less strict vows to follow.

10 Respect for Life

One of the 'Three Jewels' that Jains have to follow is 'right conduct' (Samyak Charitra). This helps to free their souls from constant reincarnation. One of the most important ways in which they can save their own souls is by not harming any other soul in the universe. This includes the souls of all people and every animal and plant. This is because every single soul has the same value in the eyes of Jains and so they should all be treated equally. The most important way in which this is done is through non-violence (Ahimsa). This means that Jains should avoid harming any living thing and should do all that they can to protect living things and the environment.

Mahavira said:

Do not injure, abuse, oppress, enslave, insult, torment, torture or kill any creature or living thing.

Ahimsa

For Jains, Ahimsa (or non-violence) affects every part of their lives. This means that every Jain must be a strict vegetarian. It also means that they should take care to avoid harm in everything they do from preparing meals to getting dressed, cleaning their homes and deciding what jobs they are going to do. Jains try to avoid wearing clothes that have been made by hurting animals such as leather or silk. They also try not to do any jobs that may cause harm to other living things. This can include working in circuses or zoos, being a butcher or a blacksmith, and selling weapons or pesticides.

www.learnjainism.org

Avoiding Violence

Some Jain monks cover their mouths to prevent harming insects and other small creatures when they talk.

Jains know that it is impossible to live their lives and avoid harm to living creatures. Simple acts such as walking down the street or having a shower will probably mean that another living creature is harmed in some way. The important thing is that they are alert at all times and the harm that Jains do to other living things is not done deliberately. Also Jains should be aware that they will probably cause harm to other creatures and must do everything that they can to avoid this. Ordinary Jains should not harm insects, animals and other people. Jain monks and nuns take a vow to avoid harming all living things.

Doing Good

Setting up animal shelters, like this one for old and abandoned cows, is one way in which Jains practise non-violence.

Ahimsa is not just about what Jains should not do. It also encourages Jains to live in a positive and useful way. This means that Jains should always practise forgiveness towards others. They should also show tolerance towards people who are different to them, give what they can to charities and work for peace and for the protection of the environment. For instance, Jains have set up hospitals and sanctuaries for injured and unwanted animals.

12 Scriptures, Myths and Symbols

Like all of the world's great faiths, Jains have symbols to represent the most important part of their beliefs. These symbols are important because, until very recently, only Jain monks were allowed to read holy books. This meant that symbols were used to remind ordinary people of the most important parts of the Jain faith. Symbols can also help Jains remember how they should live their lives. Jains also have many stories that are told so that people can understand better what Jains actually believe in.

The Jain symbol is used by all Jains and was created to celebrate the 2500th anniversary of Mahavira achieving liberation.

The outline of the symbol shows the shape of the universe. The seven hells are at the bottom. The middle part is the earth and the planets. The top of the outline is heaven.

The Jain Swastika is a reminder of the cycle of reincarnation. The four arms of the Swastika tell Jains that they will be born again in one of four realms: heavenly beings; human beings; animals and plants; or hellish beings. Jains believe that even heavenly beings will be born again.

The dot inside the crescent is a Siddha. This is the name for a soul that has achieved liberation.

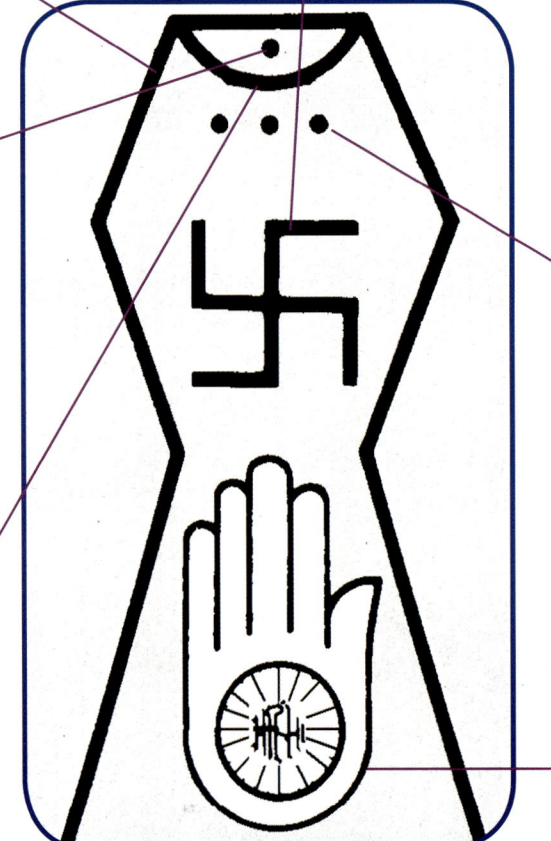

The three dots above the Swastika are the 'Three Jewels' of Jainism. These are 'right faith', 'right knowledge' and 'right conduct'.

The small crescent at the top of the symbol represents the abode where all the souls that have achieved liberation eventually arrive. These souls are free from birth and rebirth.

The raised hand means 'stop'. The word in the wheel is 'Ahimsa'. Both of them remind Jains to think twice before doing anything.

Jain Scriptures

Svetambara Jains believe that the teachings of Mahavira and other tirthankaras are recorded in a set of holy books called the Agamas. These were composed from the period 500 BC onwards. They were memorised by monks and passed down orally until about 500 AD when they were written down. The Digambara Jains believe that many of the teachings of Mahavira were lost and they have a smaller set of scriptures.

The Dreams of Mother Trishala

One of the best-known stories that Jains tell is about the dreams of Mother Trishala. She was the mother of Mahavira, the last of the

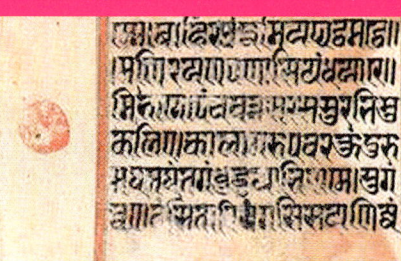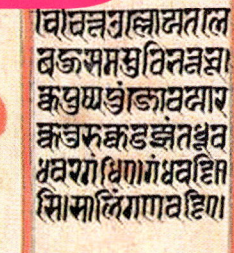
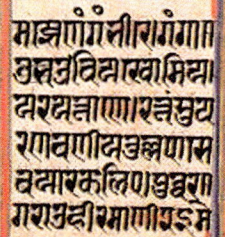

These pages from a Jain scripture show the dreams of Mother Trishala

tirthankaras. Just before he was born Trishala had 14 vivid dreams in one night (the Digambaras believe that she had 16 dreams). She woke her husband and told him about the dreams. In the morning he summoned some wise men and asked them what the dreams meant. They told him that each of the dreams showed something about the kind of person Mahavira would be. For example, she dreamt about an elephant. This told her that Mahavira would have a strong character. She also dreamt about a golden vase full of water. This meant that Mahavira would be perfect and full of love for all living things.

14 Holy Days and Festivals

Just as Christians have Easter, the Jews have Yom Kippur or Muslims have Eid, Jains also have special holy days. These are days in which Jains either carry out special rituals at home or in the temple or they gather together for a festival. Some of the most important of the Jain holy days and festivals are 'Mahavira Jayanti', 'Paryushana', 'Diwali' and 'Mahamastakabhisheka'.

Mahavira Jayanti

This is a celebration for the birthday of Mahavira. It takes place during March or April. It is believed that Mahavira was born on the 13th day of the brighter half of the lunar month of Chaitra. Jains will gather together to listen to readings about Mahavira. Images of Mahavira will also be carried through the streets.

Paryushana

Paryushana is a time for Jains to think about their faults, to ask for forgiveness and to find ways to live their lives better. It takes place in the month of August or September. This is in the middle of the monsoon season in India so it is a good time for Jains to stay at home. Jain monks and nuns do not travel during the monsoon so people have more opportunity to learn about Jainism from them. Paryushana lasts between eight and ten days. The final day is called 'Samvatsari' (the Day of Forgiveness). Every Jain is supposed to ask for forgiveness from everybody they think they have harmed over the past year. They say 'micchami dukkadam' to each other. This means 'forgive me if I have harmed you'.

During holy days the statues in Svetambara temples are richly decorated, often with precious jewels. This is the image of Mahavira at the temple in Potters Bar, Hertfordshire.

www.learnjainism.org

Diwali

The festival of Diwali is most often seen as a Hindu festival. However, it is also celebrated by Sikhs and Jains. Jains celebrate Diwali as the day Mahavira's soul left his body and achieved liberation. Hindus, Sikhs and Jains all light lamps at home and in their temples. Neighbours get together and offer each other sweets and there are often firework displays. However, Jains try not to use fireworks as they may harm living things. Diwali is very popular with Indian children because they are given sweets and presents and are given new clothes to wear.

Mahamastakabhisheka

This is one of the most spectacular of the Jain festivals. Every twelve years Jains gather in a place called Sravana Belgola in the south of India. They go there to celebrate the life of a famous Jain called Bahubali. He was the son of the first Tirthankara, Adinatha. Jains go to a giant statue of Bahubali. The statue is over 18 metres tall and is more than one thousand years old. Jains pour large jars of liquid turmeric and other substances over the statue. They place offerings at the foot of the statue. Rice flour, milk and sugar cane juice are poured on to the head of the statue. Jains believe that the ceremony symbolises different virtues of the Tirthankara's life. It last took place in 2006. Digambara Jains belive that Bahubali was the first man to achieve liberation.

The statue of Bahubali. The people above his head are pouring turmeric over the statue.

16 Pilgrimages

Many of the world's great faiths have pilgrimages. This is when people travel to important religious places to pray and worship together. Jains have several important places of pilgrimage. Although it is not compulsory for Jains to go on a pilgrimage, it is still important because it helps to purify their souls. Pilgrims also donate money to the poor and to those who help animals. Most of the centres of pilgrimage are temples that have a link with one of the tirthankaras. People going on a pilgrimage also try to take on some of the lifestyles of Jain monks and nuns.

Sravana Belgola

Although this site in the Indian state of Karnataka is used for one of the most important Jain festivals it is still a place of pilgrimage when the festival is not taking place. The statue of Bahubali is believed to be the largest single-stone free-standing statue in the world. Bahubali was a prince who gave up his power and wealth to follow a simple life to purify his soul of all karma. Digambara Jains visit his statue and lay offerings at his feet.

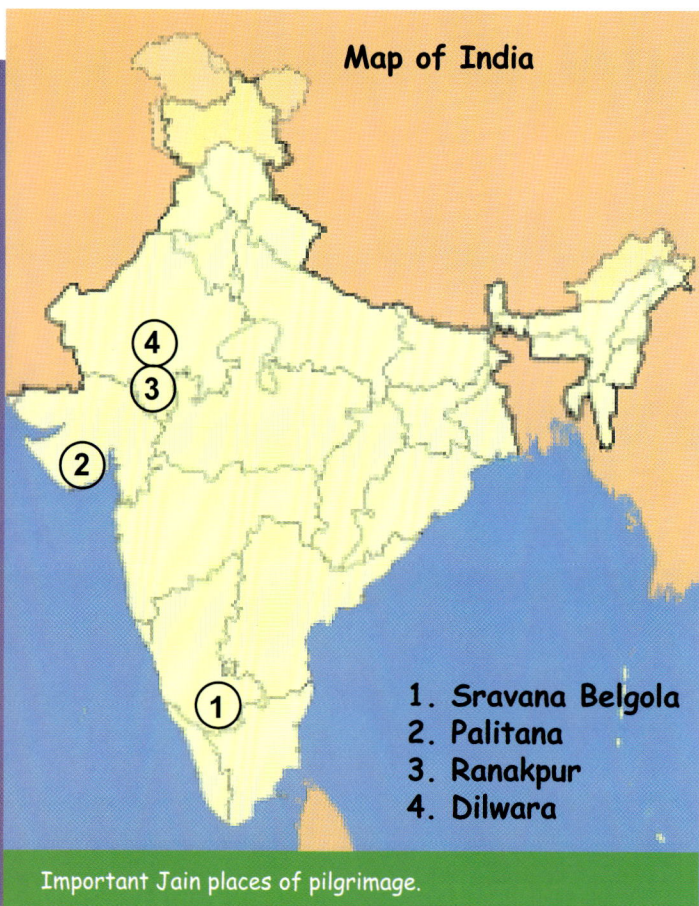

Important Jain places of pilgrimage.

1. Sravana Belgola
2. Palitana
3. Ranakpur
4. Dilwara

Palitana

Palitana is in the Indian state of Gujarat. There are over 1000 temples there. Most of them are carved out of marble. The main temple is dedicated to the first Tirthankara, Adinatha. Jain pilgrims must walk barefoot over 3000 steps up a mountain to reach these temples. They are not allowed to eat or to carry food with them. Nobody can stay in the temples when it is dark.

Ranakpur

The temple at Ranakpur.

The Jain temple at Ranakpur is in the Indian state of Rajasthan. It was built during the reign of the local king Rana Kumbha in about 1439. The halls and the domes in the temple are supported by over 1400 pillars. Each of these pillars has been carved with decorations and no two pillars are alike.

Dilwara

There are five important Jain temples at Dilwara on Mount Abu in Rajasthan. The oldest is the Vimal Vasahi Temple. This was built in about 1020 and is carved out of white marble. It is best known for its carved circular ceiling and for the shrines that have statues of all the tirthankaras. The other four temples were built between 1230 and 1582. All of them have beautiful statues and carvings.

The interior of one of the temples at Dilwara.

18 Temples

Whenever Jains go to worship at a temple their worship is very different to the kind of worship that happens in a church, synagogue or mosque. The main difference is that Jains do not believe in a god that created the universe. When they pray and worship they are worshipping the qualities of the tirthankaras. This does not mean that they believe that the tirthankaras have become gods. Instead Jains concentrate on the virtues of the tirthankaras to help them to follow their example. In this way they will be able to free their souls of karma.

Different Temples

Jain temples range from the immense and elaborate like the temples at Palitana and Ranakpur through to simple rooms with very little decoration in them. Digambara and Svetambara Jains decorate their temples in different ways.

The Jain temple in Potters Bar, Hertfordshire.

Digambaras have statues of the tirthankaras in their temples but these are not painted or decorated. Svetambara temples have statues and images that are highly decorated. The tirthankaras are painted and have gold and jewels attached to them.

www.learnjainism.org

Priests in Temples

The altar at the Potters Bar temple.

Some Svetambara temples do have priests in them. However, they are only there to help people with their worship rituals. They never lead in any prayers or any other kind of service. Some temples have assistants called pujaris. Their job is to make sure that ceremonies are carried out correctly. Pujaris do not have to be Jains themselves in order to do this work.

The Ceremony of the Eightfold Puja

This is one of the most important of the ceremonies that take place in Jain temples. It involves worshippers making offerings to an image of a tirthankara. The idea of the ceremony is that worshippers are giving up some of their possessions as offerings. Before they enter the temple Jains must wash themselves and put on clean clothing. Once inside the temple they should say 'nissihi'. This means 'giving up' or leaving behind their everyday world. They are now ready to stop thinking about the world outside and focus on their worship. The worshipper then walks three times around the tirthankara. This reminds them of the 'Three Jewels' of Jainism. They then make eight offerings to the tirthankara. These include water, flowers and incense. Uncooked rice grains are then arranged into the shape of the Jain swastika.

20 Worship

Jains do not just carry out their worship in their temples. Jains should take part in some kind of worship in their everyday lives. This is for the same reason as worship in the temples. The worship is not directed towards any god but towards the tirthankaras. When Jains pray they are not asking for anything but are just trying to find some inspiration for the right way to live their lives and to remind themselves of the teachings of Mahavira. Jain prayers can be said in any language but are usually said in an ancient language called Prakrit. Along with prayer Jains must also fast. This means going without food either completely or just leaving out certain foods. Fasting is a way of purifying the body and soul.

The Daily Prayer

One of the most important prayers is the Namaskara Mantra. This praises the five great beings of Jainism. It is said first thing in the morning and last thing at night. It is also one of the first prayers that Jain children learn.

The Namaskara Mantra

Namo Arihantanam
Namo Siddhanam
Namo Ayariyanam
Namo Uvajjhayanam
Namo Loe Savvasahunam
Eso Pancha Namukkaro
Savvapavappanasano
Mangalanam Cha Savvesim
Padhamam Havai Mangalam

The Namaskara Mantra (Translation)

I bow down to all Arihantas (the tirthankaras in the universe)
I bow down to all Siddhas (the souls who have reached nirvana)
I bow down to all Acharyas (heads of the monastic communities)
I bow down to Upadhyayas (teachers of scriptures)
I bow down to all the Sadhus and Sadhvis (monks and nuns)
These five salutations destroy all sins.
Of all things auspicious, this prayer is foremost.

Prayers and Meditations

Jains are supposed to spend at least 48 minutes every day meditating. This means that they should sit in silence either studying the teaching of the tirthankaras or thinking about how they can improve their lives. Jains should also say a daily prayer ritual called the Pratikramana. This is a prayer to ask forgiveness for any sins committed during that day and night.

A Verse from the Pratikramana

Khamemi savva jeeve,
savve jeeva khamantu me,
mitti me savva bhuesu,
vaira majjha na kenai

A Verse from the Pratikramana (Translation)

I forgive all living beings
May all living beings forgive me
All living beings are my friends
I have enmity with none

Fasting

Fasting is very important for all Jains. Fasting can take place at any time during the year. However, most Jains will fast during holy days or festivals. One of the most common times for fasting is during Paryushana. This takes place in the monsoon season in India and is a time when Jains think about their faults and how they can improve on them in the future. Fasting can mean anything from avoiding all food and drink through to giving up favourite foods. Jains must also stop wanting to eat. If they continue to want food then the fast would be pointless.

How Long do Jains Fast for?

Fasting can mean eating a little less at each meal, or eating a limited number of things in a day. It can also mean not eating at all and just having purified water. During Paryushana, Jains fast for up to 10 days. Some Jains fast for up to 30 days on only water. Others fast for a whole year, eating every other day.

22 Monks and Nuns

Many of the world's faiths have monks and nuns. These are people who have decided to dedicate themselves to living their whole lives according to the ideas of their faith. Christian and Buddhist monks and nuns live in groups to practise their faith. Jain monks (Sadhus) and nuns (Sadhvis) also do this. They live in small groups of four or five. They spend their days in meditation, learning scriptures, fasting and helping teach others about Jain truth. There are some differences between Svetambara monks and nuns and Digambara monks. The main one is that Digambara monks are naked as they believe that they should own no possessions at all, including clothes. Svetambara monks and nuns as well as Digambara nuns are allowed to wear white cloth. All Jain monks and nuns have to take five 'great vows' (Maha Vrata). These are non-violence, truth, not stealing, chastity and non-possession.

Non-Violence (Ahimsa)

All Jains have to avoid violence and harm to all other living things. This is the most important of the five 'great vows' that Jain monks and nuns have to take. However, some Jain monks and nuns take this vow much further than ordinary Jains. They either cover their mouths or even wear masks over their mouths so that they do not accidentally breathe any living things. They also carry a cloth or feather broom with them. They may gently sweep the ground in front of them as they walk so that any living things are moved out of the way and not trodden on.

Jain monks and nuns are not permitted to stay in any one place and so walk from one place to another since they cannot use cars.

Truth (Satya)

Jain monks and nuns must remain truthful at all times. This means that they have to avoid any emotions such as fear, pride, jealousy, anger or greed that might lead to telling a lie. When Jain monks and nuns tell the truth they have to make sure that the truth that they tell is good and helpful. If the truth is hurtful or causes anger then they should be silent.

Not Stealing (Asteya)

For Jain monks and nuns stealing does not mean just taking somebody else's property. It also means taking anything that does not belong to them like finding a coin on the street. For Jain monks and nuns stealing also means taking more than they actually need or having something that they are not allowed to own.

Chastity (Brahmacharya)

Jain monks and nuns have to live pure lives. One of the ways to do this is not to have any kind of relationship with others. Jain monks and nuns can never marry or have children of their own. It also means that they should avoid any kind of pleasure from their senses such as listening to music or eating tasty food.

Non-Possession (Aparigraha)

Jains believe that the more things a person owns then the more likely they are to become greedy, selfish or violent. For Jain monks and nuns this means that they should have as few possessions as possible. Digambara monks are allowed a small broom of peacock feathers and a water pot. Svetambara monks are allowed three pieces of white cloth, a woollen broom and begging bowls. Jain monks and nuns rely on donations of food and other items in order to survive. Because they have no possessions they wander from place to place except during the monsoon when they remain in one village or town. They usually sleep in temples or community halls and since they cannot own bedding, they must sleep on the ground.

A Jain nun packs her clothes and bowls. Monks and nuns carry all their possessions with them as they travel from one place to another.

24 Jainism Today

The Jain faith has survived and prospered since at least the life of the last tirthankara, Mahavira. This makes the Jain faith at least 2600 years old, although it is probably much older than that. In that time the number of Jains has always remained very small (about 10 million worldwide today). However, Jains have not only had a huge influence on the history of India but have also inspired many people in the modern environmental movement and in the vegetarian movement in India. The Jain belief that all creatures should be treated with equal respect and the fact that they try to use as little of the earth's resources as possible could make the Jains the most 'green' of the world's faiths. Jains can now be found in many parts of the world because people from India have moved to start new lives.

Jains and Indian Independence

From the middle of the 19th century India was ruled by Britain. At the start of the 20th century a growing number of Indians began to demand that they should be free of British rule and become an independent country. One of the leaders of the Indian independence movement was a man called Mahatma Gandhi. While some Indians wanted to fight the British, Gandhi believed that India could become free by passive (or peaceful) resistance. He called this 'satyagraha' (which means 'holding to truth'). Although Gandhi was a Hindu he was influenced by the Jain belief in Ahimsa or non-violence. India achieved independence in 1947.

Mahatma Gandhi, leader of the Indian independence movement.

Jains Around the World

It is difficult to find out how many Jains live in different parts of the world. It is believed that there are more than 50,000 Jains living in the United States of America. Many of them work in engineering or computing. There were also many Jains living in East Africa. This is because in the middle of the 19th century many people from India moved to East Africa to start new businesses. In 1926 the first Jain temple was opened in Nairobi, the capital of Kenya. There is still a small Jain community in East Africa.

Jains in Britain

There have been people from India living in Britain since the 18th century. However, it was in the 1950s and 1960s that many more

Jains celebrating Diwali with a play about Mother Trishala's 14 dreams at the Millennium Dome during the millennium celebrations.

people from India, Pakistan and Bangladesh came to settle in Britain. There were probably Jains amongst them. It was only in the 1970s that the number of British Jains began to grow. This was because the Indians in East Africa came to Britain to escape persecution in Kenya and Uganda. Today there are about 30,000 British Jains. They live mostly in the cities of Leicester and London. There are also Jain communities in Coventry, Manchester, Northampton, Birmingham, Leeds and Luton.

Glossary

Agamas
The name given to the Jain set of holy books.

Ahimsa
This is the Jain belief in non-violence. For Jains this means avoiding harm to all living creatures. For this reason Jains are expected to be vegetarians.

Ceremony of the Eightfold Puja
An important ceremony that takes place in a Jain temple. Worshippers make offerings to images of tirthankaras.

Digambara
One of the two main sects of Jainism, whose monks are recognised by their nudity.

Diwali
The festival of light. Jains celebrate this as the day on which Mahavira achieved nirvana.

Jiva
The soul of a living thing that will move from one body to another.

Karma
This is a substance that sticks to the soul (Jiva). Jains try to live good lives so that the amount of karma on their soul goes down.

Maha Vrata
The five 'great vows' taken by Jain monks and nuns.

Mahamastakabhisheka
One of the most spectacular of the Jain festivals. It takes place every twelve years at Sravana Belgola in the south of India.

Mahavira
Mahavira was the 24th and last of the tirthankaras.

Mahavira Jayanti
The Jain celebration for the birth of Mahavira.

Moksha
The liberation of a soul from the cycle of birth, death and rebirth.

Namaskara Mantra
A prayer that is said by all Jains at the start and the end of the day.

Nirvana
The state in which there is no karma attached to the soul and so it is freed from the cycle of birth, death and rebirth.

Paryushana
A period of eight to ten days during the Indian monsoon when Jains think about their faults and ask forgiveness from everyone that they have harmed.

Pujaris
Assistants at Jain temples. Pujaris do not have to be Jains themselves.

Samyak Darshana, Samyak Jnana and Samyak Charitra
The three ways or 'Three Jewels' in which Jains can remove karma from their souls. These are 'right faith', 'right knowledge' and 'right conduct'.

Siddha
The name for the soul that has got rid of all karma and resides at the top of the universe.

Svetambara
One of the two sects of Jainism, whose monks and nuns are recognised by their white clothes.

Swastika
A symbol of the Jain faith. It reminds Jains of the cycle of reincarnation that everyone has to go through.

Three Jewels
The three principles by which all Jains should live in order to remove karma from their souls.

Tirthankaras
These are the 24 teachers of the Jain faith. The first was called Adinatha and the last was called Mahavira.

Find out more

Websites

http://www.learnjainism.org
The website that goes with this book. It has activities on Jainism, stories, places to visit and teachers' notes.

http://www.jainology.org/
The website of the Institute of Jainology, publishers of this book.

http://www.bbc.co.uk/religion/religions/jainism/
An extremely accessible introduction to the Jain faith with some material on Jains in Britain.

http://www.cs.colostate.edu/~malaiya/jainlinks.html
An excellent introduction to Jainism with links to many other Jain websites.

http://www.sacred-texts.com/jai/index.htm
Downloadable Jaina Sutras (holy books).

http://en.wikipedia.org/wiki/Jainism
General information about the Jain religion.

http://www.oshwal.org/oshwaluk/
Information on the Jain temple in Potters Bar, Hertfordshire.

http://www.jaincentre.com/
Information on the Jain temple in Leicester.

http://www.youngjains.org.uk/
The website for young Jains living in Britain.

http://www.jainworld.com/
General information about the Jain religion.

Books

None of these books are suitable for younger readers. They can be used by teachers to find out more about the Jain faith.

Aidan Rankin - The Jain Path (O Books, 2006)

Paul Dundas - The Jains (Routledge, 2002)

P. Jaini - The Jain Path of Purification (University of California Press, 1979)

Places to Visit

The Victoria and Albert Museum, London
This museum contains a large number of Jain objects and works of art.

The Jain Centre, Leicester
The Jain Centre has the first consecrated Jain temple in the western world. Visitors are welcome to look around both the temple and the Centre.

Oshwal Centre, Potters Bar
A new temple that was opened for the Jains of London in August 2005.

The British Museum, London
The British Museum has a large collection of Jain objects and manuscripts on display.

Chester Beatty Library, Dublin
The Chester Beatty Library exhibits manuscripts from all of the faiths of India, including Jain art.

Oriental Museum, Durham
Part of the University of Durham, it has a small collection of Jain manuscripts and paintings.

Ashmolean Museum, Oxford
The Indian art galleries have some Jain pictures on show.

© Institute of Jainology 2006, all rights reserved.

First Published 2006

Typeset by	Caprin Printers Ltd Hertfordshire, UK	Illustrations	Potters Bar temple images courtesy of Oshwal Association of the UK
Printed by	Hindi Granth Karyalay Mumbai, India		Images on page 4 and 7 copyright V&A Images/Victoria and Albert Museum, London
Published by	Institute of Jainology Unit 18, Silicon Centre 28 Wadsworth Road Greenford, Middlesex UB6 7JZ, UK www.jainology.org enquiries@jainology.org		Image on page 23 courtesy of Claude Renault
ISBN Number	978-0-9554839-0-5		

The publisher would like to thank the following for their assistance in this book:

The staff of the South Asia Dept., V&A, London
The Chandana Vidhyapeeth School, South London
Ruth Ogden
Tejas Udani
Mark Rattray